MONEY IS A DEFENSE

The Revival of Biblical Stewardship

by John Sidney Martin

Unless otherwise noted, all Scripture quotations are taken from the King James Version.

MIAD Publishers 1106 Curtis Ave Joliet, IL 60435

This book and other MIAD Publishers books can be found at www.getmiad.com

Also, available at amazon.com and other retail outlets.

ISBN 978-1-948422-10-9
ISBN 978-1-948422-23-9

Printed in the U.S.A

Proverbs 6:6

MIAD's Ant Logo symbolizes the strength and the duty of
MIAD HOLDINGS LLC. Like lady wisdom, the ant of Proverbs
6:6 is also depicted as female whose ways are wise.
Understand the meaning of team and the power of
community ants forge their way in this world. Only their
creator need give them anything. They go out every single day
of their lives and work for their futures.

Table of Contents

Acknowledgments

I would like to acknowledge God my Father, from whom all blessings flow; Jesus, who is the Christ and the Son of the Living God whom by His own precious blood, has given me the victory again and again; The Holy Spirit, without which I could not have received of the LORD, this assignment that was first given to the churches nor survived the tests the accompanies the call.

I want to thank my Pastor Apostle Nona Parker, who has and still is, skillfully forged me in the fire of God's Word; Dr. Paula Price, who has been an instrument of God to keep my family and me in destiny and educate the body of Christ; my parents Titus and Mary Gibert, who helps keep my family strong and are great examples of love for God and each other to my two daughters.

Also, all of you who have allowed me to test these principles on you and encouraged me to do so all along the way. And are still supporting this effort to this very day. You know God and I know who you are.

Dedication

I would like to dedicate this book to My wonderful wife, Alvaun Yonii Martin, and my two lovely daughters, Sydnie Alvaun Martin and Saundria Alysse Martin. These three, through all the trials and tests, never wavered their faith in our Lord and King Jesus Christ or in me. The sacrifices that were made and the price that was paid for this revelation was felt by them first. They were the first partakers of all my failures, and there were many. So, by right, they must be the first recipients of all my successes. I love you three more than you will ever know, this side of glory, and more than this life itself!

Foreword

The prosperity movement that hit the church in the 1980's left prosperity in the pulpit but poverty in the pews! No one got rich except the preacher!!! But God is reviving and overhauling this spiritual move of prosperity! Jesus is gathering the "Repairers of the "Breech" to bring His truth regarding wealth, finance and mammon! Stewardship and management will be the spearhead of this move! Those that will work within the laws of prosperity (such as the ones found in 3rd John 1:2) will be made fat. Those that continue with their "something for nothing" mentalities will remain poor in all things!

Apostle Nona Parker
Pastor (Antioch Christian Assembly Church Intl')

Preface

Please read this book prayerfully. The topic of money is not an easy topic to discuss and has always been off-limits in some circles. My goal is to inform and educate you as to what the Lord has shown me concerning His financial future for all of those who would choose to be a part of it. We are on the cusp of a seismic change in the way finances around the world and in God are to be handled and managed. No longer is God interested in the so-called prosperity gospel. Jehovah is now investing in the posterity gospel. The gospel that was initially given to the churches that secures God's ownership of the earth and displays His providence in the earth to all generations through the wisdom of Biblical Financial Stewardship.

"For the promise is unto you, and to your children, and to all that are afar off, even as many as the Lord our God shall call." Acts 2:39 KJV

Introduction

What is MIAD? (M.I.A.D) Money is a Defense

"Avoiding this, that no man should blame us in this abundance which is administered by us: Providing for honest things, not only in the sight of the Lord, but also in the sight of men." **2 Corinthians 8:20,21 KJV**

MIAD Holdings LLC is a Biblical Financial Literacy Company and a Private Sovereign Wealth Fund. We are on a mission from Heaven to fight poverty and eradicate lack by teaching and training the hidden wisdom of Biblical Financial Stewardship. We not only provide the education and the training our members and clients need but we also provide the economic vehicle to help put what they learn from us into practice immediately. We get them on track to becoming the best financial stewards of their God-given resources that they can possibly be. Strictly using biblical principles hidden in the Word of God as our road map to abundant living in Jesus Christ.

We believe that the Bible is the infallible Word of God and the best resource for financial wisdom. We teach, train, and collaborate with churches, ministries, businesses and institutions that have the same vision and mission.

MIAD members enjoy a safe and secure way to save and invest money while implementing what they have learned from our programs. All the while, instilling the extremely valuable and very important personal accountability portion that is almost always missing. Membership includes an all-access pass to a wealth of biblical financial wisdom and information that we generate each day that cannot be found anywhere else. Our approach to finances is second to none. We have multiple ways to help you get the answers you need as to why you are where you are financially and spiritually. Also, how to get you where you need to be. It does not matter how little or how much money you make or have in the bank; if you're not using it as prescribed by the Word of God, you are missing the mark. Our money, or the lack of it, needs to be managed how it was created by God to be managed or money will manage us.

M.I.A.D is an acronym for "MONEY IS A DEFENSE" pulled from the book of Ecclesiastes 7:12 *"For wisdom is a defense, and (money is a defense) but the excellency of knowledge is, that wisdom giveth life to them that have it." KJV*

MIAD's goal is to focus all our investment opportunities and strategies around the acronym (H.E.E.E), which stands for Housing, Education, Economics and Entrepreneurship. We believe these are the building blocks and backbone of any thriving and developing nation of people. These goals are designed to preserve our member's capital using a biblical financial principle called (The Storehouse Principle) that is proven to provide a healthy financial future through our Private Sovereign Wealth Fund affectionately known as "The MIAD Fund."

We also service individual and institutional investors that desire to contribute to the overall positive economic growth in their own communities and within the body of Christ. We seek to create long-lasting relationships that have a tremendous economic impact and long-term value for our investors. Impact that serves the companies we invest in and the communities in which we work well. We will do this by using extraordinary people to drive the company's vision and mission using flexible capital to help "Solutionairies" solve problems.

We have determined to become the Ministers of Finance and the National Treasury for Christianity and the body of Christ. We believe that Christianity is not a religion but a Nation of Kings and Priest unto our God.

"And hath made us kings and priests unto God and his Father; to him be glory and dominion for ever and ever. Amen." Revelation 1:6 KJV "And hast made us unto our God kings and priests: and we shall reign on the earth." Revelation 5:10 KJV

"Christianity is not a religion but a Nation of Kings and Priest unto our God."

Every nation has a god. Every god has a treasury that controls that nation's wealth. Therefore, every nation must have a physical National Treasury as well. With your help and prayers, we will build The National Treasury of the Christian Nation whose God is Jehovah and whose Son is Jesus Christ. Through MIAD the world will benefit from the revival of biblical financial stewardship in a way that will create a new commonwealth to help everyone who wishes to be a part of heaven's economy which is how God dispenses Himself to humanity.

After being in business for almost seven years at the time of this writing, we believe with all our hearts that this is the will of God for His people for this time. We have prayerfully and carefully developed a set of biblical financial products that complement each other in every way possible. Starting with our signature "STOREHOUSE" account, which is designed to put more than 13 biblical financial principles into play; immediately after becoming a participant. Our Giving & Receiving accounts ensure that you have set aside funds to be generous to the poor and the less fortunate. It is also for investing in one of our many upcoming kingdom projects. Then there is the MIAD National Treasury created to store and dispense heaven's wealth in the earth in a Holy Spirit lead way to our optional savings accounts designed to help you save for just about anything. Whatever the need, we believe we can accommodate you with the right financial solution.

I have a saying that I have been trying to disprove ever since I first started saying it. I used to feel a little weird when I would say it, but one day I realized that the conviction I felt was not coming from the Holy Spirit but from the person(s) whom I had said it to. Those who I could spiritually discern, did not agree with the fact that money and finances could be so important or play such an important role in the life of the believer.

"If The Money Ain't Right, Ain't Nothing Right."

I know this is a strange and a hard saying but time and time again it has served me well when working with someone who fails to understand their problems tend to always have something to do with their mismanagement of their finances. Their lack of money was the often the main reason they also lacked options needed to be overcomers in Jesus Christ.

"A feast is made for laughter, and wine maketh merry: but money answereth all things." Ecclesiastes 10:19

It is my prayer that you will get something out of this book series that will stir you up to the point of making changes in your life that effect your eternal position in Christ Jesus. And that change happens not only in God's will but His way.

"TO LOVE GOD, WE MUST BE TAUGHT AND LEARN WHY AND HOW TO HATE MAMMON. THIS IS A SPIRITUAL MANDATE AND BIBLICAL ABSOLUTE." JSM

Chapter ONE

How It All Began

"Go to the ant, thou sluggard; consider her ways, and be wise." – Proverbs 6:6 KJV

It all started one morning in November 2012, when I had just arrived home to our tiny two-bedroom basement apartment from my regular morning routine of transporting my family to school and work. As I entered the apartment, closed and locked the door behind me, I turned on the television as always just for background noise as I prepared to start my day. As the television came on, the morning news was showing teaser stories for the next segment of what was about to be the featured stories when they came back from commercial break.

I watched intently just as the reporter of the very last teaser said, "seven out of ten people are living paycheck to paycheck with little to no savings". For some reason, that statement hit me like a ton of bricks as I slowly began to melt like ice into my living room sofa, with a look of shock and despair on my face, and with just minutes to get myself coherent before they came back from commercial break, I tried to shake myself out of it. This statement had forced me into a sunken place in my mind and soul. What was I to do with what I had just heard? It was though I felt dead, but yet more alive, than I had ever been at the same time. It was all so surreal.

I felt as though I had just been diagnosed with a common form of cancer, and that the doctor would be back shortly to give me my plan for treatment. I had no idea that I was about to hear the reporter say that this is a crisis of epidemic. Also, that the government had to figure something out quick to get people to save more for things like emergencies and retirement.

It was at that point I began to experience a deep sadness that can only be described as Godly sorrow. This is a type of deep spiritual hurt; not for the people that the reporter was describing, but for how Jesus Christ felt about the problem and how this was a tremendous disappointment for Him. As I thought about what the news reporter had said, I thought about all those people who, just like me, were toiling their way through life just accepting the bouts of poverty and lack as part of God's plan for their lives. Just hoping for the best and that somehow it will all work out in the end according to God's plan.

Then, in an instant, I came to the end of myself. I prayed and cried out to God, "Lord, how does this happen?" In the back of my mind, I was thinking to myself that this was not just me, but most of my friends and many of the people that I knew and came across on a day to day basis. As a career law enforcement officer, I saw so much poverty every day.

Then, after what I can only describe as a beautiful and powerful visitation from Heaven, the Lord Jesus Christ Himself appeared to me right there in that same small two-bedroom basement apartment. From that experience, I received not only my life's call and assignment, but also my life's purpose from the Lord.

For the rest of my natural life, I was to help as many people as I possibly could, get free from the mindsets that hindered God's ability to provide for them the way He had initially planned and still really desires too. This was to happen by teaching people all over the world about the Wisdom of Biblical Stewardship and the proper management of all their God-given resources.

Not knowing how and where to start, I defaulted to God's Word, the Bible, and began to devour any and every scripture I could about money and the wisdom that surrounded it. What I discovered blew my mind and angered me at the same time. I was in awe of God's wisdom and how he not only set up wisdo to guard riches and protect wealth, but how He also assigned a principled spirit called mammon to enforce the rules of His wealth through what's called stewardship. The proper management of someone else's or another's property.

For months, I did not even know how to articulate what the Lord, by His Spirit, was downloading into my spirit. Bit by bit and piece by piece, the puzzle started coming together. No, not how to get rich or stock pile large amounts of money for myself, family, and friends, but why He created money in the first place and its intended and unintended uses. But, most of all, I did learn, that money was a defense.

"For wisdom is a defense, and money is a defense: but the excellency of knowledge is, that wisdom giveth life to them that have it." Ecclesiastes 7:12 KJV

3

MONEY IS A DEFENSE

Now, this meant that I needed to begin my research by taking a hard look at what society historically and currently taught about money and finances as compared to what the Bible teaches. There was absolutely no shortage of sources or so-called financial experts to learn from. I had my pick and sampled them all — both Christian and Non-Christian alike. But I ran into a snag, one that I had not expected. One that would prove to be my biggest challenge. But a challenge that I would grow to love and become very good at. Revealing truth.

You see, there was a third source of information that had to be looked at an analyzed as well. This source was very powerful and had its own sets of rules for the uses of money that was being taught and promoted in various ways also. This newfound source was non other but the Modern Christian Evangelical Church itself.

There was this movement in the protestant church. A gospel that had been preached over twenty plus years affectingly coined the Prosperity Gospel. It was a gospel being propagated by many of the most significant church leaders of the times in all of Christendom. A Gospel that, in a nutshell, said that If you give God your money, He would somehow, through various ways, give more of it back to you, and as a result, you would be prosperous and wealthy. There was no shortage of flashy expensive taste preachers and pastors to keep this gospel going at full speed, leaders who made unprecedented claims as to how God was obligated to bless you and made no claim of how you were obligated to steward the blessing.

There was obviously something more missing from this gospel. Only the preachers themselve and those around them, got rich and wealthy. They used this wealth to buy more houses, cars, and planes. They built larger churches and filled them with thousands of money prospecting Christians.

Christians that show up to church week after week just to, in some way, get what they thought was a blessing. It became Casino Church.

They claim all would be well if you just kept giving, right? Wrong. I watched as many of us would bite off more debt than we could afford, and the saints gained and lost houses, cars, and filed for bankruptcy repeatedly. Something was clearly missing. Don't get me wrong! God was no doubt in this move because there was no other way to explain some of the things that were happening. From debt cancellation to miraculous financial breakthroughs, although He may have given it, many had no idea how to keep it because they could not steward it.

My research continued and I then found myself as an ex-police officer putting my investigative skills to good use one more time. Like with all investigations, there is an understanding that there are three sides to every story, just like there was in this case. First, is the complainant's side. This is the person or entity, making the claim that a crime or violation has been committed. Second, there is the defendant's side. This is the actual person or entity that is being accused of a crime or violation. Third, there is the truth. Now the truth had to stand alone on its own two feet to help solve any case and to hold up in the court of law. It was common to hear my veteran training officers say this, particularly on domestic calls.

"There are three sides to every story; your side their side, and the truth, and I'm here to find the truth."

This is exactly how I felt when I discovered that the world, the church and the bible all taught different principles concerning money, and the proper management of it. What I was hearing coming from the pulpit all my life about money was often in stark contrast to what I had studied in the book of Acts Chapter 2. How at the formation of the first-century church, those who believed, experienced a complete change in their hearts and understanding as to how money was to be handled and used? How they went from being owners of possessions and pursuing material things to sellers of those same possessions to steward the needs of their fellow believers. The bible records that they no longer felt like owners of any of their possessions any longer. What changed? Something changed. They went from an ownership mentality to a stewardship mentality in an instant, just by receiving the indwelling of the real and authentic Holy Spirit.

"And the multitude of them that believed were of one heart and of one soul: neither said any of them that ought of the things which he possessed was his own; but they had all things common." Acts 4:32 KJV

All I heard from the prosperity gospel was get money, and when you do, break God off His. This presented a problem for me because I now found myself cringing every time I would hear someone preach or teach something about money that simply wasn't accurate. Never even hearing the word stewardship or what it even meant to God.

Imagine how shocked I was to find out that there was more to finances in God than just being a tither and one who gives offerings to God through the church. Imagine how it felt to discover that the world in many ways understood money and the spirit of mammon much more than we, the church. What Jesus Christ said in the book of Luke was completely right.

"And the lord commended the unjust steward, because he had done wisely: for the children of this world are in their generation wiser than the children of light." Luke 16:8 KJV

Just think about how hard it was for me to realize that neither the world nor the church at this point cared about how shocked I was or how I felt either way. That it would not be until I could prove my findings in a tangible way; what my research was telling me was just that; "telling"! It was not until I could give people an experience that would engage all five of their senses such as: touch, taste, hear, see and smell, that they would begin to believe that the LORD OF ALL has always had a better way to manage anything called "STEWARDSHIP."

We live in a generation where people have been conditioned in so many ways, for so many reasons, because of all the social media sales pitches. The problem is not the conditioning that they are receiving but more with what they're receiving and from whom. It seems that most people today, especially Americans, feel that how to spend it is all the financial education they need to know. That money and financial literacy, even from a very early age, is not that important.

Experts are saying that our money habits are fully developed and cemented in our character by the time we are in the seventh grade. This would make the average child in America around the age of 12 or 13. This is the age when they have learned most of what they know about money by observing the way a parent or guardian handles money. As we age, people start believing that they know everything they need to know about money, when in fact, all they really know is how to spend it. Spending money is often only taught to children not by direct learning, but by observation. Children learn much more than we think they do early on by just

7

watching everything that's going on around them. This means that if I am to be effective in my call in any way, I would have to start with the family unit, the place where it all goes down. Realizing that to see change in the House of God, I would have to impact the households that make up the body of believes.

"The IRS reports that nine out of ten American households do not have access to more than four hundred dollars to navigate a family emergency."

Reports like this one and others added fuel to the fire that was already burning on the inside of me and was getting hotter and hotter with every new piece of information like this. Armed with the full understanding of my mission, I set out to find like-minded people, who I could learn from as well as teach. Whether it would be to tell them about what I had discovered about biblical stewardship or just necessary money managing skills to help with their finances. What I learned as I started promoting my message was mind-blowing.

I learned that most people don't like talking about money at all, especially when it comes to how they chose to spend it. Talking about pulling teeth! And guess what? Church folk can be the worst. Don't take my word for it. Try it yourself. Start asking your church friends if they have a storehouse or any type of emergency fund. And if they say no, ask why and then physically brace yourself. Just start poking around into your friends and family's finances, and you will have a fight on your hands. Some will manifest Mammon before your very eyes.

The only ones that would open up about their personal financial habits were those who were in deep financial trouble for their poor money habits, and were extremely desperate for my help. It did not matter what their age, gender, or station in life was. Money is not a beloved topic as television, movies, and rap videos would have us to think. The world will have us believe that it's ok to mention money as often as we would like, but not ok to learn anything about it from an in-depth spiritual perspective, although money is just that, a spirit.

For many, money is a deeply personal topic of discussion, and if you don't know someone all that well, then it may be totally off the table altogether. You may have heard that it was just religion and politics that were non-starters, well, add money to that list for a lot of people. Now I understand why offering time at church is the quietest time of the church service.

As I began calling friends and family and forcing them to listen to me ramble about my revelations, I realized that what I was saying had no weight at all until I could first prove to myself that all the financial principles I was finding in God's word worked for me first. With the evidence in my bank account. What the Bible says about money and the proper management of it had to be vetted as truth. Especially with the millennials, aka, the show me generation. So, I decide to give it a break, and I went on a six-month journey with what I had learned and had been shown by the Holy Spirit of God, how God had opened my eyes and turned my life from the power of Satan unto the knowledge of Himself. So that I might receive forgiveness of my sins and an inheritance through Christ Jesus. Six months later, I had all the ammunition I needed to proclaim God's word with confidence concerning money, and the biblical principles found only in God's word to be true with measureable results.

I went from a paycheck to paycheck lifestyle to being able to do a few things that I had not been able to enjoy in a long time without going completely broke and in debt. Or from having something taken away and turned off due to nonpayment. People began to take notice that I wasn't as stressed and had more wiggle room in my budget. I could take my family out to dinner again and buy all of us new clothes again from time to time. I even could afford to bless people again, which had been my method of operation for a very long time. So, this time around, I had a little more confidence in my voice, and I had the promises of God's supernatural provision by way of a biblical understanding of stewardship that caused my better money management skills to shine like a new penny.

I would always say to people, "You don't have a money problem you just have a lack of understanding of how money works". There was now a newfound pep in my step, and my voice carried a little more weight of glory. I could not thank God enough, and all I wanted to do is talk about money and how the Lord owned it all. I would tell people that God knows we need it, but He has strict rules and guidelines set up that we must follow to get what we need. More importantly, and to keep some of it.

"You don't have a money problem you just have a lack of understanding of how money works".

At this point, the Lord had not given me any revelation on who the spirit of Mammon really was. Of course, I saw him mentioned in scripture, but I have never experienced him or his power so I thought. I didn't realize that he had always been there from a child, when I first understood what money was.

Then one day, I was introduced to Mammon the god of money. It was not anything like you would think... Where Jesus goes "Hey John! I would like you to meet Master Mammon." We would shake hands and then exchange pleasantries. It was more like a totally unexpected illness that sent me into the hospital, which kicked off a series of financial events that had me homeless, living in a seedy hotel room with my wife and two daughters in a matter of weeks. You see, I had discovered a principle in God's word called the STOREHOUSE PRINCIPLE. The storehouse principle is a spiritual blessing on your natural resources, causing them to grow exponentially. Most understand a blessing to be God giving you something that you need or want. Although this does happen, the actual definition or meaning of a true blessing is the supernatural multiplying of something that you already have. This comes with a deeper understanding of God's wisdom that is a mystery to even most Christian leaders. I had the audacity to start putting this principle into practice, along with several others who I had convinced to save money earmarked as a storehouse with me.

Why in the world would I not think for even a moment that there would be no spiritual opposition or repercussions to what I was doing? Both Mammon and Satan had a stake in my eyes, staying shut to the truth of God's word concerning stewardship. They profited off my blindness to the highest degree. Now, I'm alive to tell you that it is never safe to assume that spiritual wickedness in high places won't come for you and your family because they will. So, you need to be prepared. You need to be ready.

I felt like Job in the Bible, where it says that before one servant could finish telling him all that he had just lost there was another servant interrupting them to describe another calamity that had befallen his household. I mean, I lost everything in a New York second. I could not make ends meet to save my life. I woke up every day feeling like a sack of bricks was there to hit me on the top of my head, again and again. All my savings were gone, and expenses were piling up. Then pow! I'm in the hospital with some sort of weird growth under the left side of my jaw, which years later, would be discovered to be a non-cancerous tumor. By this time, my little group savings fund had grown to twenty plus members with more than twelve thousand dollars in holdings, but I was paying a high price. A high level spiritual war had broken out in my life.

Both people and money were coming in from every direction, but my personal life was being destroyed, one calamity at a time. It didn't hit me that I had been served notice of encroachment by a master spirit until things had gotten so bad that me and my family were now living in the basement of the church. I was so focused on learning everything I could about money and mammon that I was losing touch of everything else. When you have an experience like I had with the Lord Jesus Christ, keeping a work-life balance becomes more and more difficult. All I wanted to do is spend time in His presence and glean from His wisdom, but I somehow had to figure out how to find and keep a roof over our heads and the bills paid all while running a growing group savings fund.

That's when my pastor called me into her office one Sunday after church and said to me. "John, this is looking really bad. I believe that you have grabbed the tail of a dragon". That was the moment I understood why everything was happening to me. Now it suddenly made perfectly clear sense to me. I could not figure it out before. It was like I was in a daze of denial. All I knew was I had not sinned and that I was trying to do the right things. The fund was growing by leaps and bounds, and God's people were becoming greater stewards, lifting themselves out of the "paycheck to paycheck" lifestyle "one by one." It was a beautiful thing to behold. But the dragon, aka MAMMON, was on my trail like a blood hound. We had just started giving out small loans to each other that helped members start businesses and buy houses. We paid off payday loans and upgraded our vehicles. Everything around us was changing and for the better. Most importantly our attitudes began to change. All things became possible if we only would believe. But Mammon would not give up. I could not make a mistake or else he was there to exact his penalty in real time. All because money became a defense and the saints prospered.

The church's tithes and our offerings started to increase, and people had money in their pockets. And here I was as about as down and out as down and out could get — not the best poster child for the seemingly successful fund manager. However, I kept pushing and trusting that Jesus was Lord and that He was on to something with MIAD Fund. Something big..

During this time in my life, I suffered more health problems, but the Lord brought me through with flying colors. The blessing was that I was not only insured, but I had full coverage by Blue Cross Blue Shield from both my jobs. So, this meant that even though I had thousands of dollars of surgery, I never owed a dime. MIAD was still going strong, and the principle of the Storehouse was in full effect. Similar scenarios were occurring in the lives of all the MIAD members with similar outcomes. The Word of God was right, 'Money Is a Defense." And we were living proof of it. Time and time again, when any situation arose, we defeated it with our defense systems wisdom and money, aka The MIAD Fund. I called it MIAD Fun.

One day I said to myself that if I had really started a war with a dragon named Mammon, then I better find out who this dragon is and what more this dragon might be capable of. I mean if he could, with a snap of a finger, cause me to lose everything, then it might be worth my while to investigate him just a little farther. This was the beginning of a whole new world for me. It was like starting all over again. Everything I had studied and learned up until that point was out the window as the Lord called me into a deeper dive, into the world of a spirit called Mammon. What a deep dive it would be! This is when I read the book Money Is a Spirit, by Dr. Paula Price. From that book, I learned that Mammon was not just a mythical character in the Bible but held real spiritual significance and played a significant role in my walk with the Lord. But when I put my hand in the Lords unchanging hand and took a walk with Jesus into Mammon's world, I found a never-ending eco system of spirits that were all created by God for His purposes, who all served Him just like Satan and Mammon unwillingly.

It was on this journey that I realized that Satan played just a part in a bigger stage play where there are many players and many roles. When I saw this, I could not wrap my mind around just how big of an operation that the Kingdom of God really is. I had been saved by God's grace all my life just to enjoy life in God. But after my conversion and my born-again experience had taken place, I could now see the kingdom and boy was it altogether different. The vastness of His wisdom and the unsearchable understanding of His love caused me to feel inhuman. Not in a wrong way, but in a superhuman way. He had loaned me the partial knowledge of who He was and what it was that I was to do for Him. I say loaned because there is always the opportunity to deny Him just like so many others have but are still forced to serve His purposes even in their condemned states. His grace and mercy kept me from the same fate.

It was from this experience MIAD Holdings became official. After all I had been through, I figured if I was to be punished for something I was doing right for the Lord, then for the life of me, bring it on! I incorporated the fund, grabbed a tax ID number, opened several bank accounts and hit the gas. I opened my big mouth and let the saints have it. All under the watchful eye of my leader, never letting myself get too far out there, of course. I learned from each experience and devoured "book after book" on money and business. I was holding myself accountable to the same word and wisdom of God that I was preaching to everyone else — making corrections and adjustments all along the way to the glory of God.

The Lord really had to deal with my heart during this period of my life because the more I understood, the angrier at myself I would get. I would think to myself "YOU FOOL"! Why have you let yourself be tricked out of God's best for your life all these years? Why have you struggled and toiled for no reason just to fulfill the lust of the flesh, the lust of the eyes, and the pride of life?" The devil had pulled a trifecta on me. He had successfully used his powers to get me to chase the gifts, and not the giver. And not only that, but he had successfully teamed up with Mammon to make it all happen. This was when I realized that the forces of darkness really are not divided, and that they work together to bring about the mastery and, ultimately, the death of our souls.

I hired someone to draw up the paperwork as well as contracts and continued doing everything in my power to thwart Mammon's power over God's people. I took hit after hit in my own finances and personal life to do so. However, who knew but God? Nothing else mattered. I was walking in purpose, defending the kingdom and its citizens just like I did when I was a Police Officer and how I still do every single day.

I gave not one bit of thought about how much I was suffering because, after all, I was on a mission from God, delivered to me personally by Jesus Christ himself. I guess from the outside looking in, it was not suitable for everyone else to see me and my family go through our get through. But that didn't matter.

You see if anyone desires to do something great and be great in the kingdom of heaven, you can bet your bottom dollar you're going to go through the fire. And that's exactly how I looked at it. People would look at us like we were on fire, but I would look at them like but see! We might be burning but we are not being consumed. I knew in my heart of hearts that God was working on a greater weight of Glory in our lives and that one day, I would be afforded the opportunity to take down one of His biggest enemies, Mammon. Knowing full well that he would not go down easy, but also knowing that somebody had to give it a try. After all, I was already a dead man walking with nothing to lose. After my last surgery, I was totally being kept alive by the pacemaker installed in my chest. But God!

So, I kept the course and carried my cross because in the middle of all this I had been working two jobs. Because of my law enforcement background, I had always been able to command a higher salary. I was now paying a sizable school tuition for my daughters to attend a good Christian school which was the original straw that broke the camel's back.

But, shortly after I got the second job it happened. The world calls it the tipping point, but the Bible calls it the day the blessings start chasing you down. In an instant, everything changed. Armed with a brand-new outlook and perspective on money and finances, I crushed it. I quickly eliminated all my debt and doubled down on my storehouse savings. Then the Lord started replacing all the things that I had thought the devil had stolen. What it really was, was all the stuff the devil, through Mammon, had given me. He just took it back. Once you change masters, you change possessions. So, God will put you in a new car and a new house with new everything. So, don't fight the loss of anything during your transition period.

I was fully restored, just like Job in the bible. I had a newer car and a brand-new motorcycle where before I was riding a borrowed bicycle to work. I could once again afford to travel and take family vacations. Boy, travel I did! I was saving money at an alarming rate, and MIAD was taking it in faster than I could loan it back out. Then about four years in, the Lord spoke to me and told me to put the company into what's called a free fall. I didn't understand it at that time, but later it would prove to be the reason that I can even write this and other books.

That's when I experienced Mammon's power in a whole new way. I did not know why the Lord wanted me to do this because, based on my research, this was not a good thing. It would be like sabotaging my own company by becoming somewhat negligent concerning its health and growth. But I was obedient and took my hands off the wheel and let the company begin to run itself.

I stopped following up with people and halted all proactive measures. Little did I know that I would learn more about money and the spirit of Mammon during this exercise than any other time. This would become extremely invaluable to MIAD's future. I learned more about how people related to, and manifested the will of the spirit of Mammon, not just money. How we live our lives thinking we are handling just paper money as a medium of exchange and not with a mastering spirit that governs its distribution and uses. Many of you reading this now will be forced to admit that this will be the first time you have ever heard of such a thing called Mammon, or given who mammon was much thought. Don't be alarmed. I had been a church boy almost my entire life and had no clue.

This was a tough time for me as manager of the MIAD Fund. Not because my baby was underperforming, nor because all the good that the fund had been used for was now becoming a distant memory. But because it looked as if it was failing and it wasn't, but optics are everything in today's world. The fact that we used the monies to do so many wonderful things was in the rear-view mirror now. Member after member began taking their monies entirely out of the fund and parting ways with us. After all, once the feel-good stories stopped, what was the reason to continue investing? Once everyone had been upgraded in their personal lives, and they were now armed with all the information they needed to maintain their status, it was a wrap. I saw this as a positive and a negative.

MIAD members now understood how to keep their expenses low and their bills paid on time on their own without me standing guard over their financial lives. Everything came to a screeching halt, and the fund's deposit balance began to drop like a hot rock. There was now, for the first time in the funds short history, more money going out of the fund than coming in. I kept faith with all diligence, knowing that Jesus Christ had a plan, and a very big one at that.

I stayed the course and noted everything that I saw and everything that happened because of the free fall. I then understood why it was vital to use the free-fall method to test your organization's ability to function without you guiding it every step of the way. A good leader must be selfless.

This book will give you a snapshot into some of what I learned along the way and hopefully you too can learn everything you need to know to get off to a great start with money in the Kingdom versus Mammon in the world. These truths found in this book is just a precursor to what is coming. MIAD or Money as A Defense is on the cutting edge of events that are about to unfold. The rise of Biblical Stewardship where Steward Kings will take their seats and drive out evil from under the sight of almighty God in heaven through the righteous Biblical stewardship of Money/Mammon. Doing completely away with what the bBible tells us is the root of all kinds of evil, the love of Money/Mammon. He who has mastered you will master you no more. Behold, God is about to do a new thing, and I believe that MIAD is going to let Him.

Fast forward to today where we have now launched MIAD 2.0 and have begun building the treasury of Heaven. With the ultimate goal of using our wealth to promote God's goodness in the earth. Sure, the Bible says that with love and kindness, He has drawn us (Jeremiah 31:3), but the same Bible says that "it is the goodness of the Lord that leads men to repentance (Romans 2:4)". Gods providence is evident through the scripture. His desire to take very good care of His sons and daughters are bragged about, even through the book of Revelations.

God has undoubtedly shown us His goodness over these last several years. Not because He has given us an enormous amount of wealth and money in the bank, but because He has entrusted us with the formula to be able to gain this whole world without losing our souls. For what really shall a man give in exchange for his soul?

It's time that someone starts the conversation about what is to be done with the over 400 scriptures that deal directly with money in the Bible. What do we make of all the parables that Jesus Christ Himself spoke and used stewardship, money, and finances to support His message and to describe the nuances of His Fathers Kingdom?

Or what about all the references made about the different churches found in the book of Revelation having become wealthy and finding themselves in need of nothing? I believe that it is high time that Christians all over the world take some responsibility for the evil in this world due to our failure to manage our Father's resources appropriately. It is the Christian Churches monumental failure to teach not only Christians, but the entire world how not to love money as the precursor to genuinely loving God. This has directly created most, if not all, of the perpetual evil that we live with in this world today.

I am almost sure what I just said will ruffle some feathers, to say the least, but for me, that would be a good thing to get you to really look at what's happening today as the partial fault of the church, not just the direct result of other types of sin. If we can do this, we can face the reality that for much of the last 50 to 60 years, the church, in many ways, has stuck its proverbial head in the sand and looked the other way when the major events that have shaped our world repeatedly happened because of the love of money.

From the Johnson Amendment of 1954, named for Lyndon B. Johnson, who introduced it in the Senate in 1954, nine years before he became president. It bans all tax-exempt nonprofits which include churches and other houses of worship, as well as charities from "directly or indirectly" participating in any political candidate's campaign.

This amendment was critical to the church financial future and its ability to become a true economic power. It promised to give the church a non-exempt tax filing status from the Internal Revenue Service. All the churches had to do was to agree not to get involved with politics. Pastors and church leaders all over the country fell for this lie; hook, line, and sinker. The sad thing is churches were already tax exempted by the constitution; therefore, did not need any other legislation on the issue.

This amendment was financial in nature and an indictment of the America Christian Church. The fine print would prove to remove much of heaven's legal rights to bless the church, and make her profitable because she had just married Mr. Non-Profit. It time for the entire body of Christ to repent and return to our first love. And began to do the things that strength us.

Over the next few chapters, I will attempt to reveal to you just enough information about what it takes to get started on this journey of awareness of God's true economy and just how He dispenses Himself to those who would share in the everlasting life that was purchased for us with the precious blood of His Only Begotten Son, Jesus Christ.

Let's dig in and dine on the word of God with the faith and hope to receive His Truth, Knowledge, Wisdom, and Understanding about the proper use and management of what we call money. In doing so, I believe that your life is about to change forever for the better. The truth of God's word will come in and illuminate your mind if received with gladness and joy.

This is what's so amazing about the MIAD Fund. Not only does it put all the right financial fundamentals in place in your life, it also aligns you with Heaven's fundamental authority to restore and resupply everything that is lacking. It brings about a financial balance in a way that only Biblical Stewardship can.

God puts His super on your natural. When we are building storehouses and other types of accounts that are in lockstep with His word, He blesses our efforts with more of what we have. This is the mystery of supernatural wealth in God. This means our focus should be on increasing what we have, not dwelling on and worrying about what we need. This, along with a business mindset, is the kingdom of Heaven's formula for wealth and abundance. When we are supernaturally increased in goods, it goes without saying that a portion of those goods are for replanting and then daily consumption. Then we are to give away a portion to those who might have need, selling what's left for a profit, and starting the process all over again and again. This is to be done in a proper fashion and in this specific order, so that the perpetual blessing flow can in and out of our lives like a river. It's when we rearranged this order that things began to happen out of our control. God is the God of order because order sustains, preserves, and makes alive. This is what this book and MIAD is all about. Bringing biblical financial order back to the body of Jesus

Christ. Giving them that believe the ability to once again take no thought for their lives and to seek the kingdom of God first.

OWNERSHIP VERSUS STEWARDSHIP

Chapter TWO

It All Belongs to God

"The earth is the LORD'S, and the fullness thereof; the world, and they that dwell therein." - Psalm 24:1 KJV

One of the most important facts that anyone who desires to fulfill their life's calling in God, no matter what it is, this you must learn to recognize and acknowledge that God (Jehovah) is the only creator. Making Him the rightful owner of everything. Without this truth being securely fastened to your spiritual foundation, you will have trouble contending with the spirit of Mammon, or any principality for that matter. At the end of the day, He owns it all.

"In the beginning, God created the heaven and the earth." Genesis 1:1 "For by Him all things were created, both in the heavens and on earth, visible and invisible, whether thrones or dominions or rulers or authorities-- all things have been created through Him and for Him." Colossians 1:16 KJV

Without first acknowledging this fact fully and accurately, one cannot move into a position of power or true authority on the subject matter. Therefore, the effects of what this book offers you will be diminished to a few good ideas and formulas. It is the faith in knowing that we don't own anything that qualifies us for more.

To help you understand this very vital principle, I direct you again to the book of Genesis Chapter 1.

"So God created man in his own image, in the image of God created he him; male and female created he them." Genesis 1:27 KJV

"And God blessed them, and God said unto them, be fruitful, and multiply, and replenish the earth, and subdue it: and have dominion over the fish of the sea, and over the fowl of the air, and over every living thing that moves upon the earth." Genesis 1:28 KJV

In verse 27, we see that God created man male and female, and he gave them an assignment, or job if, you will. But in verse 26, he describes in detail how HE (Jehovah God) was the creator of everything that is on earth, above and beneath the earth. This means as the creator He is also the owner of what He created. By right, anyone who creates anything from their own imagination, strength, ingenuity, and resources are automatically responsible for that creation as the original source.

From birth, we spend a great deal of time proving to our parents that things we can't even pronounce yet are ours. We learn to cry like the dickens every time someone removes our binky or bottle. At the first opportunity, we start to voice the word "MINE". Full ownership of everything is in the heart of a child from their sin nature.

As part of this fallen nature, we are born with the DNA of the thief. We are raised to own and care for our possessions out of a sense of ownership, never giving it a second thought that naked we came into this world and naked we will leave it. It is not until we receive the pure Word of God and the indwelling of the real Holy Spirit that we began to really understand and realize that we own nothing but only possess that which the Lord has given us. The story of Job who was rich in every way came to the same conclusion after losing everything he had and becoming physically afflicted, he began to cry with new understanding.

"And said, Naked came I out of my mother's womb, and naked shall I return thither: the LORD gave, and the LORD hath taken away; blessed be the name of the LORD." Job 1:21 KJV

The Apostle Paul who proudly called himself a prisoner of the gospel and a bond servant to the Lord counting all his worldly knowledge and possessions as dung also said,

"As sorrowful, yet always rejoicing; as poor, yet making many rich; as having nothing, and yet possessing all things."2 Corinthians 6:10 KJV

If you search the scriptures, you won't find a single verse that would suggest that God has surrendered, or turned over, permanent ownership of anything. God didn't die and leave the earth—or anything in it—to you, me, or anyone else as owners. He gave man the earth as stewards and managers of it, not as owners to the degree that He relinquished all His legal rights to it, or forfeited the right to take it back. This includes Satan, Mammon or Angels and Demons.

"The heaven, even the heavens, are the LORD'S: but the earth hath he given to the children of men." - Psalm 115:16 KJV.

The word given in the verse denotes given control over, but not ownership of. Only to havve dominion over If for a moment, we should think that we even own our ourselves.

Let's no longer make this mistake in our hearts to believe that just because we got the job that doesn't mean we own the company. When a person decides that he or she owns anything, they are displaying the character of the thief, and we all know who that is. The thief comes not but to steal then kill and then ultimately destroy what was never his to start with. So, we must guard our hearts against the theft of false ownership of God's property.

"You are not your own; you were bought at a price"- 1 Corinthians 6:19,20 KJV

It all belongs to God. You don't even own yourself. Not that this is a bad thing. But we were created to work, having the ability to manage and enjoy what we have worked for. But, as I said before, we spend a great deal of time all our lives trying to prove to the whole world that everything belongs to us. As soon as we start getting older, the phrases "My This" and "My That" becomes the most used words in our daily vocabulary. The ownership syndrome kicks in and takes over our young lives. We don't begin to learn stewardship until much later.

MONEY IS A DEFENSE

As we grow older, it becomes more and more about what we own and have full control over. We are always told all through our adolescent and into our teenage years that one day, we would be required to get a job and work to buy our own stuff. Or own this and own that. People say things like, "Don't you want to own your own home and your own car, and your own family someday"? Never are we told that ownership of anything comes with a price and a level of responsibility that we may or may not be designed for.

It is the providence of God that provides everything we see, touch, hear, smell and taste. This providence is the trait or characteristic of who He is as a Father. The word Father means "Provider". God the Father created the heavens and the earth so that He could love and provide for His creation in peace and harmony. In direct fellowship with Him as a family. This is still His desire to this day. But Satan and Mammon are in the way.

It is His natural ability and concern as a father that will not and cannot turn over ownership to anything or anyone until they have first worked for it, and secondly fulfilled all the requirements to not only prove that they should have it, but that they can also keep it. I have a saying that says, "It's not in the getting, it's in the keeping it that counts to God". And to keep something that God Himself has entrusted you with demands that you first become a winner by overcoming or beating the odds. He must first see the winner in you before He can win with you.

Jesus Christ said this: *"To him that overcometh will I grant to sit with me in my throne, even as I also overcame, and am set down with my Father in his throne". Revelation 3:21 KJV*

At this point, I pray you're starting to get the picture. A picture that probably looks much different than the one that

30

has been painted for you all your life. You know, the one that portrays mere men being the controllers of your destiny and lords over large groups of people. How government is the father of men and that they own everything, and what they don't own they can take any time they feel the need to do so. Well, I'm here to tell you that for many this is not only true; it is the only reality that most people will ever know. Most will remain blind to everything that is being forced down their throats every day by all sorts of media. Never will they take the time to go on the journey of discovering the truth for themselves. That is why we must sound the alarm. It is way past time for everyone to know that things are wrapping up, and it is now time to prepare ourselves for the final test.

It is not until you meet the King, Jesus Christ, and become familiar with His power and authority that you start to realize very quickly that there is more to the story. We now fully understand that there are levels to this game called life and that you have just been called up to another level of it. I pray that the Lord with His grace and mercy will install His spiritual and natural dominance in your heart, mind, and soul.

And suddenly you awake to the fact that other men are just that! They are men and women who, just like you, are having an earthly experience and fighting their way through it just like the next person — talking about the wakeup call of all wakeup calls. But yet, with an overwhelming joy, we are received into this new life with our Savoir, Master, Lord and King.

"I counsel thee to buy of me gold tried in the fire, that thou mayest be rich; and white raiment, that thou mayest be clothed, and that the shame of thy nakedness do not appear; and anoint thine eyes with eyesalve, that thou mayest see".
Revelation 3:18 KJV

MONEY IS A DEFENSE

There is something else of great value that we receive when we experience that saving power of the Lord Jesus Christ: the supernatural understanding of our own mortality. We begin to feel so small, or just a small piece of a much larger puzzle and plan. God designed our mortality to be a daily reminder that we do not, and I repeat, we do not, only belong to ourselves, but we cannot even control the time or day we check in out of this game called life unless we commit suicide to which there is no forgiveness.

When the proper amount of time in prayer is spent meditating on just who God is in relation to how big He is, we begin to understand His power and ability to commune with us and download information to our now alive and connected spirits.

This download of spiritual information to our souls and newly awakened spirits is a very delicate time in a new Christian's life, and it's crucial that they get a good foundation to stand upon concerning the way God's kingdom operates financially. Far too often this experience is tainted, if not destroyed, by a false gospel and arrant doctrines that teach them that God and Heaven were created for us and that Jesus Christ and The Holy Spirit of God are only here with us to ensure that we live our best lives. That all the angels in heaven are at our beck and call to serve and obey our every prayer, we pray. This could not be farther from the gospel's truth. We were created to bring God pleasure, and now we belong to Jesus Christ.

"Thou art worthy, O Lord, to receive glory and honour and power: for thou hast created all things, and for thy pleasure they are and were created." Revelation 4:11 KJV

God is God. He, being the creator of everything, thinks much different than we do. He is the center of the universe, and His number one priority is... guess who? Himself! He is the common denominator and the thread that holds everything all together. There is no one more important than Him. For without Him, nothing that is can exist. Get the point? When we rehearse these truths long enough to secure them deep down in our souls, then and only then, can we begin to even hope to benefit from what God is doing in the earth and with all of mankind.

Then can we have the hope to be used by Him to bring about His will, His way? For this has now become my life's goal to help people understand that which must be clearly understood. That like Jesus Christ, we must be about our Father's business and recover all that which was lost. MIAD is on a mission to bring about genuine change not just to the financial industry and the way Wall Street does business but also in the hearts of men and women that have been taken advantage of by Mammon and his band of thieves.

By taking our rightful place as stewards of the earth, and not owners of it, we deceive not ourselves and no longer take on more than we can handle. The life of a steward is much more rewarding than the life of a supposed owner. Sure, there are many things in life that we will have the pleasure to say we own, especially those things that we create with our own hands by making something out of nothing. But we cannot, and must not, allow Mammon to trick us into thinking that at any time we are operating outside of the providence of God and have only become the benefactor of His goodness.

Jesus Christ and the way He lived His life is the greatest example of how we are to not only think, but to also act and behave. Having the understanding to know that Jesus Christ is the author of our very life itself and the author and the finisher of our faith. He and He alone has the power to give life and take it away. We look forward to seeking Him daily for instructions on how to receive our daily bread. Placing full confidence in Him and Him alone. Being mastered by Him and Him alone. Loving God the Father and learning to hate all His enemies, including Mammon.

By doing these things we moved into a place in God that receives our lives and a fully functioning part of God's plans for the earth. We no longer are the water in the oil but now become the oil for the wine that restores souls. By placing full ownership where it belongs back into the caring and skillful hands of Jesus Christ, we fall directly into our rightful place as stewards. The day this gets into your heart, mind, spirit, body and soul will be a day that you won't soon forget. It's the perfect marriage and a match truly made in and from heaven.

No Man Can Serve Two Masters

"No servant can serve two masters: for either he will hate the one, and love the other; or else he will hold to the one, and despise the other. Ye cannot serve God and Mammon." - Luke 16:13 KJV

This passage of scripture is somewhat different from the one we find in Mathew 6:24. In the Gospel of Matthew, it reads like this:

"No man can serve two masters: where in Luke 16:13, it reads "No servant can serve two masters:" KJV

I'm not one to get super technical over word play, but I do want to point out the fact that every man is a servant. I also would like you to chew on the fact that a servant also means slave. Now, I know in the world that we live in today, most people have a huge problem with both words, servant and slave. However, the fact remains true that God created mankind to be stewards of everything He owned in the earth and it was sin that turned us into servants and slaves when what He created and wanted from the beginning was sons.

Known by many names over the centuries, the god of riches and wealth has been misunderstood and miss-characterized for far too long. Mammon's role, from the agent of God's provision, to reluctant giver and accuser must be examined further. Mammon went from the prince or principality that ensured that Jehovah's providence was experienced by everyone to quickly turning into being in direct opposition to the one that created him, yet still remains in

God's employ. He went from having the desire to show mankind God's goodness in a way that pleased God, to using his most powerful tool money, and to attempting to receive all that love and affection for himself. Have you ever known someone that disagreed with their boss but still had to keep working for them? They did the work but subverted them every chance they got. They undermined every decision and took all the glory for the victories when their boss was right. They thought in their minds that they were the real boss. But it got so bad that the day came where the line had to be drawn and the distinction had to be made. Everyone had to pick a side. Who were you going to listen to and take instructions from? The real supervisor or the one who only thought they were the supervisor?

This was clearly the case, as stated in Matthew 6:24, when Jesus Christ Himself made the distinction between His Father and Mammon being the two masters. Going as far as to say the only way to love one is to hate the other. It is taking extra precaution to include that you must despise one of them to hold or cling to the other. Topping it all off by saying, "Ye cannot serve both God and Mammon." Now, how intense is that? Here we have Jesus Christ Himself, the Son of The Living God, making a very bold statement and declaration for the ages, saying "Hey world Listen up"! There are two masters true enough, but you can only work for one, not one at a time. Mammon is the name of the one who works for the Father but thinks he is the owner of the family business. We have decided to continue to allow him to think this because it will provide us with the proof of who is with us, and who is with him.

I imagine when you hear money is a spirit and it has a voice for the first time, your eyebrows will raise up, as mine did. Remember the hit TV show Different Strokes from the late 70's early 80's? Gary Coleman was famous for saying "what you taking bout Willis" to his older brother Willis, when Willis said something highly questionable or profound. This was a way to say what you just heard makes absolutely no sense at all. But I'm giving you a chance to prove it to me. Money really has a voice. I'm sure you have heard the sayings "Money talks, you know what walk's", or "cash is king and has a voice all of its own". Well, take those cliches literally, and bam you're on your way to discovering the differences and similarities between money and the spirit of Mammon. God set this whole thing up by giving us the option to either conform to His will or go with His unrighteous substitute Mammon, and make your own way.

But don't be fooled by Mammon, because it's really a bait and switch tactic to get you to serve him and to do his will using money as the lure. Mammon would have us all believe that he is the creator of money, but he is not; he is only the prince over it. Mammon is a general. Make no mistake about that. He has a boss just like everybody else, in both the spirit and natural worlds. These seen and unseen worlds move only according to their designs and when they get off course, the creator of it all has already, in his Word, given us instructions on what to do and how to handle such occurrences.

It's through prayer that things change. Prayers are requests and/or instructions to start or stop something in the unseen world by unseen agents that go to work to produce a tangible result in the seen world. Let me show how this works in scripture, by the supernatural, through prayer and giving.

"And said, Cornelius, thy prayer is heard, and thine alms are in remembrance in the sight of God." Acts 10:31 KJV

In the book of Acts, a man named Cornelius had been praying and giving alms to the poor. That's when an Angel appeared to him as said to him that both his prayers and his giving had caught God's attention. This lets us know that these two activates are important to God. So much so, that they kept reminding God that Cornelius was available to be used for His glory. This was, in fact, precisely what happened when God spoke to Cornelius through His angel, and had Cornelius send for Peter to the saving (salvation) of his entire household.

When prayer precedes, or goes before, giving, Mammon is locked out of the equation. That's a transaction between you and Heaven that cannot be hacked. Jesus Christ put a supernatural seal on this combination of prayer and giving that is totally Mammon proof. When we learn the art of connecting our prayers to our giving with tangible results, we are provided the evidence that Mammon is not only not our master, but that we belong fully to the Lord Jesus Christ.

"And all things, whatsoever ye shall ask in prayer, believing, ye shall receive." Mathew 21:22 KJV

"The LORD shall command the blessing upon thee in thy storehouses, and in all that thou settest thine hand unto; and he shall bless thee in the land which the LORD thy God giveth thee." Deuteronomy 28:8 KJV

Here we have God commanding a blessing on His people. Do you ever wonder who might God be commanding? Take a guess. I will give you three chances, and the first two don't count. The fact that Jehovah God should command anyone to do anything is an indication that He, through His strong sovereign power and will, has given somebody or something the power to make their own choices and decisions. Now, what God do you know by name, that is so confident in Himself to do something like that, knowing full well that these self-willed beings or creatures might use that small bit of power to link up and try to do what Satan and his boys tried to do? What an awesome God, right? Why wouldn't you serve and love a God who can do this? Let me rephrase the question. Who wouldn't serve a God like this? So, Mammon must answer orders to bless God's people, and I'm sure he doesn't like it one bit. Not only because it's God's people and not his. But they hopefully know and understand that all good and perfect gifts come from their Lord, so that means Mammon gets none of the glory. But what he also hates is the fact that most the time he is being forced to bless someone that hasn't met the standards or been the best steward. This means his mandate has been overridden by the overrider.

Mammon must bless good stewards because they are following the principles of which he is the prince of, but he makes a case against unjust stewards and takes that case up before the Lord as the prosecutor and accuser armed with plenty of evidence about our financial crimes. I sometimes can hear his voice as he accuses my clients/members of money mismanagement. It was the weirdest thing to me for a very long time until I received the understanding of how the courts of Heaven worked. Although he often makes a good case, the last word still belongs to the LORD. Mercy is always available but not the ideal. Too many of us rely on, and use up more than, our fair share of God's mercy, especially where our financial management is concerned, and we all somehow know it deep down in our souls. Almost like we have a spiritual calculator embedded in us that says NO CREDIT because you are not doing this right.

So, several years ago, when I had been doing some back-alley money coaching with friends and family as my test subjects, I started to hear what sounded like courtroom banter in the spirit. As I mentioned earlier, this was before I knew anything about the courts of Heaven. For some time, when talking with someone about their finances, I would hear this voice accusing them of not doing this with their money, or not doing that. I had no choice but to write it off because I didn't understand it.

For a while, I was hearing this voice, thinking it may be my brain on playback from my law enforcement days, but that didn't hold water because the voice was accusing the person I was speaking with. So, all I knew to do was to tell them. I would tell my clients Mammon is accusing you and talking about you so don't forget to pay your bills on time. Or Mammon is trying to set you up, so be on guard and watch your money. It became one of my regular Facebook posts, "Watch Your Money People."

I would say this to encourage them not to fear what Mammon is always trying to achieve, and that's obscurity. He does not want to be noticed as he sets up his schemes and traps for all those who are unaware. He hides behind the scenes of our lives to deceive us. His name is mentioned only four times in the gospels. But now through the wisdom of God he is being fully exposed to us for such a times as this.

As time went on, and as I watched my own financial picture begin to change and change me, I realized that I had indeed been serving Mammon all those years and not God. I mean, when I began to apply the principles found in God's Word and the revelation that He gave me, at the same time my whole family experienced a shifting from barely scraping by and not knowing why, to having more than enough, and yes, even tasting an abundance. Before I decided to conduct the experiment by sending my company and my personal finances into a free fall, it was like I could have it all if I were just to start falling back into the sensual selfish side of having money.

You see, money must be appropriately handled or it will handle you. And there are many sides to money and its power is undeniable. Mammon does a pretty bang-up job getting people to tap into all the God-awful things that money can do. He can even have a person thinking about nothing but money all day and all night long. He can even have you worrying about it until you are very sick in your body and can't even sleep without medication. Many become hospitalized behind the worry over their finances, and drug addicted. You love Mammon when you love money more than God. You love Mammon when you can't love God without money.

That's the real mammon. The Mammon that Mammon doesn't want anybody to focus on. But his time is up, and he is being forced out of the shadows. The Almighty in His wisdom is raising up an army of kingdom sons that would become the stewards of His kingdom. Steward Kings! Not just in the preaching and teaching of the Word of God, but also in the marketplace where they will prove to the whole world that the earth is the LORD'S.

In **Matthew 6:24,** Jesus Christ gives us one of the biggest clues to a successful life in Him without making a big deal of it. Yet on average, you will only hear this scripture in a sermon used a couple of times in your lifetime. To this day, this is one of the most underutilized and misunderstood verses in the Bible, yet, in my opinion, one of the most important. *"No man can serve two masters".* Wow. This verse is, a foundational verse and one of those verses that if we get it right, it will set the proper course of your entire walk with the Lord. Eliminating many of the struggles that come with the lack of not just finances, but also the lack of understanding.

I will attempt to explain, as best I can, how misunderstanding this Bible verse has changed everything and how I believe that God will use this book series to fix the perception of money and Mammon by the believer. I say this because if you're not on the right path, you're going to end up somewhere you didn't intend to. In the same way that if you're not serving the right master, then you're not going to get the results the God of the Bible says you can get. Again, God set this whole thing up to prove one of two things, whether you could and would conform to His will or go with His competitor Mammon, who offers a way of using money to do your own will, thus becoming your own god. When we remove the need for God out of our lives and replace Him with money we now serve Mammon.

Now, this is not to say money is evil because in and of itself it is not. But the spirit and principality that controls its distribution is a very unrighteous spirit. We must learn to govern ourselves accordingly and manage Mammon's power over us by managing money well. Yes, the very thing that Mammon controls is the very tool we use to defend us from his control. This is simply the wisdom of God.

"And I say unto you, make to yourselves friends of the mammon of unrighteousness; that, when ye fail, they may receive you into everlasting habitations." Luke 16:9 KJV

Both verses of scripture show us that Mammon is not to be ignored, but mastered. More importantly, that Heaven looks upon our stewardship of money to determine and vet whom the Lord can trust, not just here on earth, but throughout all of eternity. This is one of the most interesting commands in the Bible. Its mind blowing to say the least, that we should seek to befriend those that serve Mammon and enter into an agreement that allows for business transaction to take place. Helping them to the point that when we run out of money, they come running to our rescue. Wow, just wow.

So, there you have it. Mammon is a master, but only because God the Father gave him the authority to be so. We need him to do his job and to do it well. I can say that having overcome him myself, I am still contending with him every single day. He is always waiting for me to color outside the lines of my stewardship and tries me every chance he gets. Being the founder and CEO of MIAD, I get the pleasure of taking some major hits, but learning from each one. My faith and resolve are getting stronger by the day. I have submitted to the Lord, like the Apostle Paul, to know what it is to lack nothing but also what it feels like to be abased and in need.

"Therefore seeing we have this ministry, as we have received mercy, we faint not;" 2 Corinthians 4 KJV

I can now with my whole heart say that no matter which scenario I find myself in, on any given day, that I am to be content just to be in the will of God. The mere thought that He, in all His power and glory, would choose me to carry the good news of the gospel of Jesus Christ causes me to tremble with fear. Least I let Him down in anyway and no longer become worthy to walk this thing out and write these books.

This gospel tells the whole story of how, from the beginning, God the Father had a need. And, that need was to be met by the creation of mankind. The need would start out as one man and one woman given the responsibility to take care of God's garden, which was a place of meeting. It was to be well kept and made to be as beautiful as possible. They would have no lack of anything to not only do their jobs, but for their own personal consumption and enjoyment.

After the fall, the Son of God, Jesus Christ came and redeemed that which had been broken and lost. Now we are once again given our original assignment with a few twists, of course. Not to steal from our Father but through stewardship, prove to Him that we are worthy to be His heirs as Jesus Christ did when he died for His Father, according to His will, resulting in our salvation of the entire world. Giving us the promise of John 3:16.

"For God so loved the world, that he gave his only begotten Son, that whosoever believeth in him should not perish, but have everlasting life." John 3:16 KJV.

No other god has done this. No other god has made claims to have died for anything. Therefore, Jesus Christ can make the statement that no man can serve two masters. God the Father, Jesus Christ the Son and The Holy Spirit has done so much for mankind that no other god could even conceive of doing. They have every right in the universe and beyond to say we refuse to except anyone who's allegiance is split. In fact, we are going to make it impossible for this to be even possible for any man to do.

This is the reason that MIAD is so critical for the times that we are living in today. We can no longer take Matthew 6:24 and Luke 16:13 for granted. Our election concerning this issue must be made sure by our actions and the proper handling and use of money. Proving step by step that our hearts belong to God and His kingdom. Refusing to allow Mammon or any other unrighteous being corrupt our souls to hell. Guarding our heart and each other with all diligence. I thank God in heaven for this day and the way of escape He has given us through MIAD Holdings LLC.

So, whatever is in store for my life, I pray "so let it be" according to what is written of me in my book in Heaven. Allowing for death to work in me so that life can work in you. Having the same spirit of faith. Know the He which raised up the Lord Jesus will raise me up also. For which cause I faint not, though my flesh is dying, but my spirit man is being fully renewed. For the trouble in life that is only for a moment, pales in comparison to what the Lord has shown me.

"WATCH YOUR MONEY PEOPLE"

John Sidney Martin

Chapter THREE

The Call Back to Stewardship

"His Lord said unto him, well done, thou good and faithful servant: thou hast been faithful over a few things, I will make thee ruler over many things: enter thou into the joy of thy Lord." - Matthew 25:21 KJV

There is one word in the above passage of scripture that is said to have been mistranslated. And that because of this error, it has changed the way many in the body of Christ see their role or position in God's Kingdom. The word "Servant" was originally the word "Steward." If you re-read the verse using the word "Steward" in place of the word servant, it makes more sense, and the picture becomes much clearer. See, servants are not stewards, but sons are stewards by default. Sons steward their father's wealth, land and possessions. Sons are also heirs of the estate.

Sons do not see their life's calling or occupation as a servant but as a steward, because sons usually work in the family business and follow in their father's skill or craft. Sons also regard themselves as future owners being that they hear their fathers continuously say, "Son one day, this will be all yours." Servants receive a paycheck and nothing more, but sons receive an inheritance and are rightful heirs to their father's estate. Servants look forward to the day that they may, by their faithful service and good stewardship, be called a son.

"Wherefore thou art no more a servant, but a son; and if a son, then an heir of God through Christ." Galatians 4:7 KJV

I once had the opportunity to work alongside the owner of the company's son. Although he was a hard worker and did the same jobs that all the other employees did, it was apparent that there was a difference between him and the other employees. He was a very humble guy and never played on his being the owner's son status, not even once. But the obvious could not be ignored because it was plain as day that one day, he would be our boss.

He did not have to prove to the other employees that he was better than any of us, nor did he walk around, beating his chest about how fast he learned the job. He simply worked with his head down like everyone else and kept his nose clean, as they say. Day after day and month after month, his true identity and his real place in the company began to emerge.

Then came the day when it was time for him to start making the shift. It was a gradual thing where he would start taking his break in the office and not with the rest of us. Then he started extending those breaks. There was a rather large plate glass window in the wall of the office area to allow them to see if we were working, but it also allowed the same for us. We noticed him getting more and more comfortable with the office staff, which was basically his father's partner, and his wife and daughter. Before long, there was a desk placed in the office for him, and it became official that he was no longer one of us factory employees, but now he would be our supervisor.

"Now I say, that the heir, as long as he is a child, differeth nothing from a servant, though he be lord of all;" Galatians 4:1 KJV

He went from servant to son to owner and heir of his father's business. Only after he had proven his ability to keep his father's business running and growing, which is exactly what he did, when he figured out a way to expand the product line, this meant new revenue for the business and major kudos for him.

This is how it works in the Kingdom of Heaven as well. We start out as servants but end up as sons and daughters after our stewardship has been proven and we have been found to be trustworthy and faithful in all our father's house. It is having the ability to keep it and dress it all over again, just like with Adam and Eve in the garden of Eden. But this time we must do this in a wicked and unrighteous world.

"If therefore ye have not been faithful in the unrighteous Mammon, who will commit to your trust the true riches?" Luke 16: KJV

We are rewarded here on earth with the fruits of our labor and the spoils but also in Heaven when we will see our Lord and Savior Jesus Christ and our Father face to face. It is our stewardship abilities that stand between our servant-hood and son-ship. Sons manage their father's estate/money well while servants only work for it. Sons have a level of sovereignty to make critical decisions given them by their fathers, while servants are hired to show up on time and do their jobs while following the policies and procedures. Then they go home at the end of their shift.

"And the servant abideth not in the house for ever: but the Son abideth ever. John 8:35 KJV

Which are you? Are you still a servant or have you accepted your position, role and responsibilities as a steward in God's house? Have you come underneath the rule and authority of Heaven knowing full well that one day you will be given your own ruler-ship? It is my earnest desire to be a faithful steward in the house of God, and over all the Lord's holdings that He would entrust to me. Having the opportunity to be found faithful over a few things and one day being made ruler over much.

"And Moses verily was faithful in all his house, as a servant, for a testimony of those things which were to be spoken after;" Hebrews 3:5 KJV

The Poor You Will Have Always! Poverty is big, big business and has been for a very long time. Some call it a war on poverty, but for centuries, the battle rages on. And although Jesus Christ created a world that houses and contains enough wealth for everyone, there are those whom wealth seems to elude the entirety of the lifespan. This is a real travesty that simply cannot be changed.

"For ye have the poor always with you; but me ye have not always." Matthew 26:11 KJV

MONEY IS A DEFENSE

Jesus Christ knew that because of the effects of sin that there would be those who would not be able to overcome poverty. That there would be conditions that were lifelong that prohibited people particularly in that time from being able to do the things necessary to escape poverty's deadly clutches. That it would be either a physical or mental hindrance caused by age such as being too young or too old to work that impairs their ability to earn enough money to build a storehouse and work the biblical financial principles that would bring them any level of sustainable wealth.

This was especially true with the widows who lost their husbands, as well as those who lost their parents and were orphaned. These two groups of people are often left without any means to generate income or wealth. For the widows who became that way due to losing their husbands to war, if they were young enough, they could often remarry if they so choose to, but many times depending on their ages they could not. This also meant that they became socially stereotyped and thrown aside by society, which means they could not gain access to the economic system of that time to make enough money to take care of themselves. Sort of like a stay at home mother who, after twenty years of taking care of her husband and children, now finds herself having to figure out how to rejoin the workforce. And as for the orphans, it goes without saying that a whole set of new challenges presented themselves every day; never mind having no guidance or real shelter.

"Pure religion and undefiled before God and the Father is this, to visit the fatherless and widows in their affliction, and to keep himself unspotted from the world." James 1:27 KJV

If we the church, the ground and pillar of truth, as the people of God, really desired to provide proof or concrete evidence that we have mastered the spirit of Mammon and overcame this world, then this is where the results are going to show up. Not in how big of a house we own, or how fancy of a car we drive, but in our collective ability to take care of those who, by no fault of their own, are incapable of taking care of themselves. Sure, there are many that do, but there are just as many, if not more, that don't. Every House of God is called to some level of benevolence.

"And in those days, when the number of the disciples was multiplied, there arose a murmuring of the Grecian's against the Hebrews, because their widows were neglected in the daily ministration." Acts 6:1 KJV

This is not to say that there are situations and scenarios in which the family of certain people should not bear the burden of their family member, but if there be no family, or any that's willing, we are to be prepared to step in and show them God's providence. By doing so, we position ourselves as an active working gear in the transmission of Heaven's economic power and to be made a witness of who He is in all His glory and kingship. Promoting His providence towards them that love Him.

"If any man or woman that believeth have widows, let them relieve them, and let not the church be charged; that it may relieve them that are widows indeed." 1 Timothy 5:16 KJV

Here we see something that is very important that we cannot miss. We see Jehovah allowing the ministering of the Apostles to be interrupted because the business of the kingdom was not being handled properly. God literally shut down the priestly duties of the Apostles until the Kingly duties got taken care of. This speaks volumes to the importance of Heaven's reputation. How miracles, signs, and wonders took a back seat to the providence of God, which was seeing to the welfare of the widows. God's credibility as a Father and provider was not to be thrown aside again.

"Then the twelve called the multitude of the disciples unto them, and said, It is not reason that we should leave the word of God, and serve tables. Wherefore, brethren, look ye out among you seven men of honest report, full of the Holy Ghost and wisdom, whom we may appoint over this business." Acts 6:2-3 KJV

Make no mistake. God cares deeply about the health and wellness of His people. Why? Because He is a King and in fact, He is the King of kings. He indeed expects those whom He has called and those that have been chosen to understand this about His character and His nature, to not forget or forsake the business side of His kingdom. Jesus didn't forget that, although He was the Son of God, He had to be about His Father's business.

The business side has everything to do with the administration of His providence. Stewardship is not just managing money and resources well; stewardship is also representing your source well. Always making sure that the recipients of God's goodness always understand fully, who and where the blessings have and continue to come from. If we do this correctly with the right heart and attitude, we will witness even our adversaries giving praise and honor to our God for His goodness, mercy, and kindness towards them through us.

I have had the pleasure and honor as MIAD manager to experience these many times, and each time is a pure joy to my soul. The original fund had several non-believers as members. Mostly people I knew from work who needed someone to hold them accountable to save. They were happy for my help because they could see exactly how far the Lord had taken me in a short period of time. It was this group of MIAD members that were the most grateful when they would find themselves in a financial bind and MIAD's services and benefits kicked in to save them.

We had one member that was so excited and grateful for MIAD that she started tithing to our church. When she called me up and said that she wanted to pay her tithes though her MIAD account I was shocked because why would she? When I asked her, who do you want to pay them to, because you have no church home? She said very boldly "to Antioch" like duh, are you stupid? I could not wait to get off the phone to call the pastor about what just happened.

Is Jesus Christ really calling His bride the church that He died for back to a place where stewardship is important? A Place where she minds the things of God and the Spirit only. A place where she can be free from the entanglements of the world. My answer to that question is unequivocally "YES". I believe this is ultimately expressed in the Book of Revelations and several of the books in the Bible that precede. In the book of James, we see this:

"Let the brother of low degree rejoice in that he is exalted: But the rich, in that he is made low: because as the flower of the grass he shall pass away." James 1:9,10 KJV

MONEY IS A DEFENSE

Throughout the book of James, we are reminded time and time again how to treat the poor and regard the rich. Admonishing the believer to not just pray for people who also have a bodily need for something, but to also supply that need; or what does it profit? Stating very clearly that faith without works is dead.

The Apostle Peter said "Be Ye Holy as your Father is Holy" and to the new born babes to desire the sincere milk of the word. John encouraged us to walk in the light, having no fellowship with darkness. Stewarding our salvation by keeping Gods commandments. Jude, the brother of James said "contend for the faith by stewarding the House of God". Protecting it from false teachers. And the called back to stewardship is all over the first three chapters in the book of Revelations.

"Remember therefore from whence thou art fallen, and repent, and do the first works; or else I will come unto thee quickly, and will remove thy candlestick out of his place, except thou repent." Revelation 2:5 KJV

Developing A Prosperous Soul

"Beloved, I wish above all things that thou mayest prosper and be in health, even as thy soul prospereth." 3 John 1:2 KJV

To prosper and be in good health. Isn't this what every human being wants? Isn't this what life on earth is all about? Was is not God the Father's intent from the beginning to give mankind His love, which resulted in goodness towards all men? Isn't this the intent of all fathers who love God? That our children learn as they grow, and enjoy all that life has to offer; being rewarded for their godly hearts and pure souls with good health and plenty of wealth?

Life is full of ups and downs, and many of them cannot be avoided. But there is a saying that sums it up perfectly. "Life is not about what happens to you but more about how you react to it." Why is it important to react to life's challenges in the right way? Because everything comes down to the condition of the soul. The soul must be reprogrammed appropriately to the original specification, before sin, in order to function correctly and the way God intended it to.

The spirit of a man received its instructions from God. The souls receive their instructions from the spirit. And the body receives its instructions from the soul. If the spirit of a man is in God, then the spirit is not the problem. But if the soul of a man is not converted to obey the spirit of a man, then Houston, we have a problem because the body is not going to get the spirit memo.

It is the soul of men that gives Heaven so much trouble. The soul being the interface between the spirit and the body is ultimately to blame for whether things go right or left in our lives. But very little to do is made of the condition of the soul. Let alone making sure that it becomes more and more prosperous. However, that's all changing because there is a genuine movement going on where God is raising up ministers that are specializing in dealing with the issue that lies deep within our souls. Some are even calling themselves "Soulologist", which I think is cool.

These are men and women of God that are often Apostles and Prophets who have what it takes to face the deeper issues contained within the soul that keep us prospering. This is done by attacking the root system of a person's soul with strategic prophetic insight and powerful Apostolic anointing's that bring about healing and deliverance.

A prosperous soul is a soul that understands that their stewardship is not just connected to the pocketbooks, but that stewardship of their souls is more important. Anyone could learn the fundamental of handling money and increase their knowledge all the way up to expert level, but if their soul is not flourishing in God, they have gained nothing. Health and Wealth are married, and a prosperous soul is a key to both.

A prosperous soul is a soul that is always learning. Not just learning to be learning; but learning the way God would have us all to learn. And that is from the perspective of knowing Him, the fellowship of His suffering and seeing life from His vantage point, being totally secure in the fact that He is God and God alone.

"For what is a man profited, if he shall gain the whole world, and lose his own soul? or what shall a man give in exchange for his soul?" Matthew 16:26 KJV

God in His great wisdom has shown us, by Jesus Christ, that there is a way to enjoy health and wealth. And that this is His desire for His Sons and Daughters. But Jesus Christ cautions us repeatedly that we must first take up our cross and follow Him. In doing so, we must deny ourselves and lose our own lives. Jesus said in verse 25:

"For whosoever will save his life shall lose it: and whosoever will lose his life for my sake shall find it." **16:25 KJV**

Developing a prosperous soul is all about devouring the Word of God so much so that your complete and total outlook on life changes to the degree of understanding that God is exactly who He says He is, and that Jesus Christ has saved your soul. Fulfilling every promise He has made.

The soul is made up of three parts. Your emotions, your will, and your intellect. All three parts must take on the same understanding that God is God, and He is everything that He says He is and much, much more.

For the emotions, that looks a little something like this; all your emotions are under the control and authority of Jesus Christ. This means that no matter what your feeling, whether in your flesh or coming from your heart, God is greater than our hearts.

"For if our heart condemns us, God is greater than our heart, and knoweth all things." **1 John 3:20 KJV**

Having a prosperous soul is when our emotions know and understand that God knows everything will be all right, no matter what it feels like at that time. Having all the faith needed to become fully aware that the answers are on the way.

Developing a prosperous soul also means no longer having a battle of the wills with God. For the truth about our human will is this; the only reason that God gave us a will is so that we could submit it to His. When His will becomes our will and our will is fully submitted to His will, then and only then, will our souls prosper in this area. When you know that all that you have come to know means nothing in relation to the knowledge of the excellency of Jesus Christ, you're getting close. Giving thanks in all and in everything we do and say. Why we must do this is simple, it's Gods will.

"In everything give thanks: for this is the will of God in Christ Jesus concerning you." 1 Thessalonians 5:18 KJV

Having a prosperous soul comes from a heart of thanksgiving. A heart of thanksgiving comes from a real understanding of who Jesus Christ is and what He accomplished on the cross at Calvary: fulfill His obedience to His Father first, and receiving a nation of people as His bride, and as His reward. When you are born again and can began to see the kingdom of Heaven, you become a part of very great. You then become so thankful for the fact that you were on your way to a devil's hell, but because of God's perfect plan and Jesus Christ's perfect obedience, and the indwelling of the Holy Spirit, you have become a partaker in an eternal covenant. Bought and paid for in full by the precious blood of Jesus.

I pray that you would take a moment and put this book down and began to think about exactly where you going to spend all of eternity. Just do yourself the biggest favor in the world and began to pray and talk with your creator God about His will for your life and how you can either get started or continue that journey. You will be so glad you did.

How Prayer Changes Everything

"Is any sick among you? let him call for the elders of the church; and let them pray over him, anointing him with oil in the name of the Lord: And the prayer of faith shall save the sick, and the Lord shall raise him up; and if he has committed sins, they shall be forgiven him. Confess your faults one to another, and pray one for another, that ye may be healed. The effectual fervent prayer of a righteous man availeth much." James 5:14-16 KJV

Prayer is quintessential to the life of the Christian. Learning how to pray is good stewardship in and of itself. Praying from your position as a good and just steward, wreaks Mammon's plans to lock him out of God's blessings for your life. I can't say enough about the level and the quantity of prayer that is needed to overcome the Spirit of Mammon and to stay his hand in your life. But I can say it will almost never be enough, and will come at a very high cost.

Mammon is one of the most formidable foes you will ever face on this side of glory for the born-again believer. I say born-again because until you have been birthed by the Holy Spirit into the Kingdom of Heaven, you will only see Satan as enemy #1. Think about it. The Bible says that Satan will flee when we resist him for a season anyway, but Mammon isn't going anywhere because money is his domain, and money is something we all need to live on this planet. To resist Mammon is to submit to a life of poverty and lack. Rather needing to resist him, we ought to fight to overcome him instead.

Jesus said unless we become born again, we cannot even see the kingdom. Once you are born again, Satan and his three-point plan of destruction becomes smaller and smaller as those that the Apostle Paul calls Principalities, Powers, Rulers of Darkness, and Spiritual Wickedness makes themselves known to you. Mammon himself, being a Principality, will be most recognizable to you because of your daily fights with him. The primary way we overcome Mammon, or any enemy of God, starts with prayer. Prayers are keys that unlock Heaven's resources and delivers them to earth.

"And I will give unto thee the keys of the Kingdom of Heaven: and whatsoever thou shalt bind on earth shall be bound in heaven: and whatsoever thou shalt loose on earth shall be loosed in heaven." Matthew 16:19 KJV

I believe God has given us access to the Kingdom of Heaven's economic system. I also believe that MIAD has been birthed into the earth as a modern-day version of that system and that it will become the blueprint needed to guide us into a more prosperous future in God by Christ Jesus. We can clearly see the pattern in scripture of how God has, and is still, using His people in the following four areas to produce and secure the wealth of His Kingdom, and to manage it in a way that produces life, and not death. Joy, and not sadness. Peace, and not war.

1) BUSINESS: As I mentioned and discussed earlier, business is war. Christians are warriors, and we must go to war. No, not the type of war where we fight with guns and knives, but the type of war called business. Business is also taking care of people. Finding out what it is that people need, and providing them with it. It sounds easy but it's not. Providing God's creation with the things that they need and want is more than a notion, and much prayer must undergird every endeavor that the believer takes up because of the spiritual warfare that is evolved. Sure, there is a type and level of business that is all-out war. I mean it is really cut-throat, and not for the faint at heart, and millions of dollars can ride on every decision. But there is also a type and level of business that is kind and gentle, yet business nonetheless. The Christian is not to shy away from either but in all things praying for peace as you execute the business plan flawlessly.

I believe that there is a businessman and businesswoman on the inside of every believer because a businessman dwells on the inside of us. If Jesus Christ is living in you, then by default, you have been reprogrammed to do our Father's business. And that is to manage His creation and manage it well.

2) EDUCATION: I cannot say enough about how important education is to the believer. Especially financial education and business management. Prayer is vital to a Godly education to gain wisdom, knowledge, and understanding of the ways of God. The word of God is full of mysteries that only open up to the diligent and the righteous seeker of its truths. This is also true of its financial truths. The monetary policies found in God's word are not to be taken for granted, least we find ourselves in the clutches of Mammon our whole life long.

"For this cause, we also, since the day we heard it, do not cease to pray for you, and to desire that ye might be filled

with the knowledge of his will in all wisdom and spiritual understanding;" Colossians 1:9 KJV

3) WORKPLACE: Let's talk about work ethic. Most develop their work ethic or the lack thereof at a very early age. Just like money handling skills, experts say that they are developed by the age of seven. This means our work ethic would generally come from our parents or guardians. Well, so did Jesus Christ. He watched His Father in heaven. And mimicked Him perfectly; claiming to do nothing that He did not see His father do first. We must develop this exact same work ethic.

"But Jesus answered them, My Father worketh hitherto, and I work." John 5:17 KJV

Jesus would later go on to say that He does absolutely nothing that He doesn't see His Father in Heaven do first. How about that for throwing distinction out the window? He also stated that He and His Father were one, which makes His strong resolve not to want to do His own thing more understandable. But, If Christ is formed in the heart, mind, and soul of the Christian believer, should we not be able to make this same boast. Not only about our own behavior but how we pray, view, and understand our role in this world. How we are to work while it's day, before the night comes, in which no man can work.

4) POLITICS: Politics is a form of business. Business through legislation if you will. Ultimately, politicians have the power to write laws and policy. So, if you want to do business at a sustainable level over a long period of time, then you must know and win the favor of them that can change things for your industry. People who are given the authority by the people who, with one stroke of the pen, can and will write you right out of business for good. Politicians are the go-between of the people and their businesses.

These three areas are key to God's agenda, in the earth. Wicked men have always known this, but now it is high time that the believer knows and understands it too. It has been the absenteeism of the church in these areas, and many others that have given this evil and wickedness to take root in the systems of this world and defile them with Satan's agenda which is to ultimately make merchandise the souls of men, working fully with the spirit of Mammon to bring about a one-world financial system.

MIAD will deploy an army of intercessors that will under-gird the company with prayer and intercession. Bombarding heaven night and day for the release of the financial wisdom necessary to turn this evil world upside down and on its ear, concerning the deeds that cause billions to live in impoverished conditions far away from the pure providence of their creator.

These intercessors will also be available to pray with the individual members on a myriad of financial topics and issues. From savings to debt issues. Student loans to dealing with inheritances. From generosity and world missions to local giving and support. Praying for our membership will become a large part of what we do as part of our daily operations. And rightfully so, because we can do nothing apart from our Father.

Restoring Biblical Financial Principles is going to prove to be very vital and essential to the reformation and the revival of the New Testament Church. We must back up and began to do what was done at first to experience what true revival is all about. Something that many have been praying for a very long time. This can only be done by the church universal sending out a clarion call to come back to real biblical stewardship — the Godly management of Heaven's holdings in the earth.

"And the Lord said, who then is that faithful and wise steward, whom his lord shall make ruler over his household, to give them their portion of meat in due season?" Luke 12:42 KJV

The biblical principles of financial stewardship can be found all over the Word of God. These principles must be explored exhaustively to identify the qualifications to be just/justified. Stewards are managers of God's property, and a good and just steward understands who they work for and exactly what their assignment is. They also fully understand that if they are faithful and wise, that one day they will be given their portion (ownership). This is something they must never forget.

From the book of Genesis, where God employed Adam and Eve to take care of the garden, to the book of Revelation, where Jesus gave His assessment of the seven churches, we see an examination of their stewardship abilities. Even Jesus Christ Himself understood that it was all about managing His Father's business and those who His Father had sent Him to save, teach, disciple, and keep them safe from hurt, harm, and danger. He knew that these men were vital to the message of the Kingdom being promoted through the world, and He did not lose any, except the one that had been prophesied well beforehand about which was Judas, the one who betrayed Jesus with a kiss. We see this in His words when He said:

"And this is the Father's will which hath sent me, that of all which he hath given me I should lose nothing, but should raise it up again at the last day." John 6:39 KJV

66

Jesus Christ gave us the best example of just stewardship. That as a just steward, you should lose nothing that has been entrusted to you. We see this play out in the parables of the minus and talents. Where both times, servants had been entrusted with their master's possessions, and in both cases, it was money. They were not only expected to preserve it, but to grow it even to the point of doubling its original value or quantity. The servant that failed to do so was banished to hell while the servants that were successful received ruler-ship and increased wealth and responsibility. Jesus Christ also showed us an example of what we all will need to be ready to say to Father when on that great day as we stand before His throne and we meet Him face to face in the following scriptures.

"Now they have known that all things whatsoever thou hast given me are of thee; 8 For I have given unto them the words which thou gavest me; and they have received them, and have known surely that I came out from thee, and they have believed that thou didst send me.;9 I pray for them I pray not for the world but for them which thou hast given for they are thine." John 17:7,8,9.

Can you at this point in your life say these things also? Can you tell the Father that you told the world what He told you to tell them? That the world knows without a shadow of a doubt that it was Him that told you? Can you say that the world has received it and now believes that you belong to God and have been sent by Him to help them? Jesus though He thought it, not robbery to consider Himself equal with God still did not cross the line into thinking that what God had entrusted to Him was owned by Him. In verse nine, He expresses this by saying that He prayed for them that had been placed under His watch and care because although they were given to Him, He understood that they belonged to His Father.

If Jesus Christ himself understood His role not just as the Son of God but the caretaker of everything God owned and placed under His care, then who are we to take this lightly? We who also see ourselves and children and/or sons and daughters of God must also begin to see ourselves as stewards and caretakers of His kingdom. Then and only then will we be able to call ourselves kingdom citizens. We cannot make the claim to be sent by God or called by God, and we do not care about stewarding His Kingdom and His people, which are also His possessions.

Biblical Stewardship must be fully restored to the body of Christ, starting with the teaching and training of all the Biblical Financial Principles. MIAD is committed in playing a huge role in seeing the entire body of believers in Jesus Christ to this end.

We are soliciting your prayers and your action. If we all began this journey to becoming the best stewards of our God-given resources, it is possible the entire world will thank us. Now is the time for this generation to make its mark. The future generations are depending on us to get this done, and it all starts with prayer. My prayer for you is that your faith fails not. And that you take a stand for the sake of history.

John Sidney Martin

"THERE IS ONLY ONE SECRET TO MONEY, AND THAT IS TO HAVE SOME; AND MY JOB IS TO MAKE SURE THAT YOU DO JUST THAT." JSM

Chapter FOUR

The Commonwealth Realized

"That at that time ye were without Christ, being aliens from the commonwealth of Israel, and strangers from the covenants of promise, having no hope, and without God in the world:" Ephesians 2:12 KJV

What is a Commonwealth? It is a community founded for the common good, such as the general good or advantage and public welfare of its citizens. In the Bible, the nation of Israel, God's chosen people, was a commonwealth nation. A nation that seeks to minister to the good and welfare of every one of its citizens equally. The type of society that man has tried to recapture ever since Adam and Eve were kicked out of the garden of Eden. A utopia if you will, where every man, woman, and child was taken care of. Not because of a government that provided everything they needed and more; but because of the God that they served, who commanded them to love and take care of one another. Preferring each other over themselves.

"By this shall all men know that ye are my disciples, if ye have love one to another." John 13:35 KJV

Many men over the centuries have tried and failed to bring this type of governing system into being without the oversight of a benevolent God. They have all failed miserably. From communism, with the promises to make everyone equal, to socialism, which is downright theft of everything, to Imperialism, and every other "ism" that you can name or think of. We, as human beings, have tested and tried them all.

Many wars have been fought, and lives have been lost to bring these ideas into fruition. Religious, political, and outright idol worship, have been the reasons to justify their existence. None have succeeded for more than a thousand years as did the great Roman Empire that was not a perfect society by any means, but somehow managed to stay in power longer than all the rest due to its military power.

Up until this very day, man has tried to bring about on his own, only what our Lord and Savior Jesus Christ can give us. That is the ability to manage God's resources in such a way that brings Him glory first and then provides for the needs and wants of each citizen in His Kingdom.

"The strict handling of money in a systematic, way based on biblical financial principles, is mandatory for every believer today without exceptions." JSM

Because money is a spirit, you cannot treat it as an inanimate object. Strict protocols must be implemented at salvation or shortly thereafter as part of our discipleship training. Money is such a touchy subject that most leaders shy away from the biblical teaching of its use, other than when trying teaching on the tithe and the offerings. Moreover, these teachings about money and finances must be valued and protected as the gospel that they are.

Money has guardians, and they only work for God. When we take our rightful place in God, they begin to recognize us and move at God's commands. They skillfully release resources to us as we increase our ability to steward them. This stewardship also includes our ability to safeguard what has been entrusted to us individually, and as a community of believers. This is where the watchmen come in. Every church has watchmen.

There are different types of watchmen, and all are very necessary to keeping the Kingdom in the hands of the right King. By protecting its citizens from those who wish to destroy their way of life. Financial watchmen are needed today more than ever before. Those who watch over God's financial interest. Those who will put His holdings as priority, now and forever.

We see a day coming where all God's children will begin to understand God's ways and how through His sovereign power, He has given us a system in which, if handled with care, produces a desired outcome, which is a community of people that love one another, free from greed and the destruction that comes with it. A community of people who lacked nothing and no good thing was withheld from them.

"Pure religion and undefiled before God and the Father is this, to visit the fatherless and widows in their affliction, and to keep himself unspotted from the world."

A people that would dare to live their lives so unselfishly that any and everyone who would hear of this great love for each other, would pray to God for an opportunity to join and become a vital part of this movement. Not just lacking no good thing, but also in any good deed that is to be done. Having a pure religion is to ensure that the fatherless and the widows are an at-risk group of people that must be guarded in a special way.

It's time to once again show the Kingdom of Heaven and all the seen and unseen worlds, the manifold wisdoms of God. How will we do this? By taking care of His business in ever sense of the word. Advancing this powerful Kingdom through stewardship, not ownership. Operating as steward kings for the King of kings.

"Neither was there any among them that lacked: for as many as were possessors of lands or houses sold them, and brought the prices of the things that were sold," Acts 4:1 KJV

It is the mission and goal of MIAD Holdings to revive and breathe the breath of life back into the understanding of our roles as stewards and managers. Then, by God's sovereign power, we pray that He would once again restore and renew a right spirit within us. The Spirit that the church received on the day of Pentecost, that would ultimately bring about a great change of heart through the conversion of our souls. Giving us that same, if not more, ability to love one towards another.

"A new commandment I give unto you, that ye love one another; as I have loved you, that ye also love one another." John 13:34 KJV

MONEY IS A DEFENSE

It is with so much excitement that I look toward the day when MIAD is operating at full capacity. I already have seen a glimpse of what I haven't seen, nor ears have heard. A glory to be revealed once our obedience is fulfilled. Tasting the joy that has been set before us that drives our willing hearts. Giving ourselves fully to God in every way. It will be His will, His way, forever and forever, amen.

MIAD Holdings in Scripture

"And not that only, but who was also chosen of the churches to travel with us with this grace, which is administered by us to the glory of the same Lord, and declaration of your ready mind: Avoiding this, that no man should blame us in this abundance which is administered by us: Providing for honest things, not only in the sight of the Lord, but also in the sight of men." 2 Corinthians 8:19-21 KJV

The Lord gave me the concept and structure of MIAD directly from Bible Scripture. As I studied The Word of God and researched all the different types of economic systems and situations in it, I found that God had a master plan. I discovered that the financial system that Heaven was trying to get to earth, wasn't about a change in money handling habits, but a change of heart.

It started on the day of Pentecost when I believe God gave the church, that was being newly formed, the economic blueprints of Heaven's commonwealth system — downloaded directly into the hearts, minds, and souls of every believer through the indwelling of His Holy Spirit. Promise made, promise kept. The power that Jesus Christ had assured them He would send, was in the planet and already starting operations. A comforter to guide them into the truth.

It was an exclusive bonus that those waiting on the promise received that day in the upper room. A supernatural economy was downloaded into the heart and soul of every believer when they all received the gift of the Holy Spirit, with the evidence of speaking in tongues and other languages.

This economy created a fellowship between them that they had never experienced before. One that caused them to want to come together on one accord, and to be there for each other as a family in every way. Therefore, a fellowship was formed, and the bibles says that, because of this new condition of their hearts, they had all things in common and they instantly shared an understanding of money and Kingdom economics.

"And fear came upon every soul: and many wonders and signs were done by the apostles. And all that believed were together, and had all things common;" 43) And sold their possessions and goods, and parted them to all men, as every man had need. Act 2:43-45 KJV

This behavior quickly formed an all-new community of Jews as they continued and remained steadfast in the Apostles doctrine. By the Holy Spirit, they began to give away and sell their excess goods and possessions, including land and houses, of which they turned the profit over to the Apostles, who gave it to those that needed it. They made it their business to ensure that no one named among them lacked anything. This oneness was the results of an instant change in the condition of the heart, courtesy of the Holy Spirit. Therefore, I wonder today if it's the real Holy Spirit that many Christians have, because of the lack of this evidence in their behavior to care about the needs of their brothers and sisters.

The Apostles went on to become the CEO's of this new upstart hedge fund that was hotter than Apple, Amazon, and Google stock combined. It pleases God so much so, that He, by His own ability, invested in His own company by adding more than three thousand souls/stewards in one single day. How about that for quick expansion? We serve a God who thinks big and plans accordingly. The Bible says this newfound love for one another, caused by the change of heart, made them no longer consider any of their possessions their own.

"And the multitude of them that believed were of one heart and of one soul: neither said any of them that ought of the things which he possessed was his own; but they had all things common." Acts 4:32 KJV

MIAD, being fully rooted in Biblical scripture, is at the forefront of orchestrating a new era of Biblical Kingdom Financial Management. One that will shift the entire Church and body of Christ on its axis. Tilting it back into a position that favors the wisdom of our Lord and Savior, Jesus Christ the King. How will we do this? With your help, of course. Are you ready for the reset?

As I continued to allow the Lord to teach me that what He was showing me was not His first rodeo. He took me into the Old Testament where repeatedly I would read, and studied all the times in which He would reset the system and turn the tables on His enemies by taking His wealth away from them.

"A good man leaveth an inheritance to his children's children: and the wealth of the sinner is laid up for the just." Proverbs 13:22 KJV

Every time the wealth of the earth would become unbalanced in the favor of the wicked, and they sought to harm and take out His regents in the earth, Jehovah would raise up a man to recover it all. He did this with Abraham and Joseph. With King David and his son, King Solomon. Then with Jesus Christ, who by the power of God, shifted economies wherever He went. And then with the Apostle Paul, called it the administration of the abundance. (2 Corinthians 8:20) Notice I said, "They made it their business". MIAD is now making it our business to revive kingdom stewardship by modeling what it looked like all throughout scripture — this time using technology and better systems to make it happen much faster and worldwide. Just Like MIAD 1.0, money was coming in from all points north. Apostle Paul perfected the previous commonwealth model by merely making it global. With the help of Titus and several other men, who were also above reproach, they managed a system of giving and receiving that was backed by a supernatural touch from Heaven.

It's this same supernatural interference from Heaven, into the affairs of men, that we expertly invite. Knowing that God's desire to show the world who He is, by His providence through His church, is just the beginning of what we are so eagerly looking forward to — Jehovah God ruling in the affairs of MIAD.

"This matter is by the decree of the watchers, and the demand by the word of the holy ones: to the intent that the living may know that the most High ruleth in the kingdom of men, and giveth it to whomsoever he will, and setteth up over it the basest of men." Daniel 4:17 KJV

Today, MIAD Holdings LLC., is strategically positioning itself to build and improve upon all the wisdom and Principles found in God's Word. To restore a level of biblical financial understanding to the earth. Through is education system, coupled with the business arm, we are uniquely being equipped by Heaven to grow in grace at a rapid pace. Our goal is to become the most significant blessing the world has ever seen, and to move the church and the body of Christ on into perfection. The zeal of the LORD shall perform this. Won't you join us in this effort and this fight today?

MIAD Biblical Foundation Principle

MIAD Holdings diversifies its holdings using four main Biblical Financial Principles.

The Storehouse Principle found in Deuteronomy, 28:8, and 2 Chronicles 32:28 KJV.

This Principle is used by the MIAD company to help our members always have something that God can bless. It is a perpetual savings account.

The Treasury System in Deuteronomy; 28:12 and Jos. 6:19-24 KJV.

This Principle is a nation-building principle of providing for the financial health of the nation of Jesus Christ. It is a leveraged money market account.

The Commonwealth Systems found in Acts 2:44-45 and Ephesians 2:12 KJV

This Principle is a system designed to track and monitor the everyday financial needs of the nation and to meet those needs that are common to everyone.

The Ministry of Giving and Receiving in 2 Corinthians 8-9 and Php. 4:15 KJV.

This Principle is a system of investing, borrowing, and lending that causes growth in the finances of the individual member from the individual members.

"IT'S TRUE WHAT THEY SAY THAT THE LOVE OF MONEY IS THE ROOT OF ALL KINDS OF EVIL, BUT I SAY THE LACK OF IT IS THE FRUIT OF ALL TRAVESTIES."
JSM

Chapter FIVE

The Conclusion of The Matter

"Let us hear the conclusion of the whole matter: Fear God, and keep his commandments: for this is the whole duty of man." - Ecclesiastes 12:13 KJV

"All is vanity", said King Solomon, the wisest man to have ever lived. He said this repeatedly. In this book, he takes us on an incredible ride through the wisdom and folly of what we call life. Solomon became the wisest man ever to have lived, having been given his wisdom by God himself. A true Godly wisdom to see life the way God sees it, and not the man-made wisdom that is steeped in sensual lust of the eyes and the flesh, and the pride of life.

Mammon, while working with other gods, desires to exploit us by exploiting our strong desire for riches and the pursuit of money, fame, and wealth. He will not stop at anything to prove that we really love him more than the one who created us. His futile effort to prove his own worth and value will be diminished by this work that we call MIAD. Just like disowned son's, Mammon and all the other gods, are in denial that they have failed and want nothing more than to destroy their replacements. In doing so, they have waged an epic war against the Most-High God and His Son, Jesus, who is His Christ. This war is played out every day in our lives as we battle to secure our place in eternity.

It is now time for the Sons of God to take their places in the earth and to begin righting this sinking ship. Pointing to a kingdom not made with hands, but demonstrating that same kingdom here on earth through mighty, powerful, and the miraculous acts of God's providence, through His Apostles and Prophets. MIAD will lead the charge economically as the treasury of the Christian Nation of Jesus Christ.

We are beginning now to see His Kingdom that was sent to earth from Heaven, become populated and occupied by a generation of people who will not bow down to fear or any of the other gods. For they shall fear God and God alone. Girding themselves up in the most Holy faith, ready to avenge all unrighteous, with their sights locked perfectly in on the thief of all thieves, Satan, who would dare steal from the great and most powerful and terrible God.

"For I reckon that the sufferings of this present time are not worthy to be compared with the glory which shall be revealed in us .19 For the earnest expectation of the creature waiteth for the manifestation of the sons of God." Romans 8:18,19 KJV

MIAD's VALUE PROPOSITION

Seven out of ten people are living paycheck to paycheck with little to no savings. 10 out of 10 say that they wish they could start saving money or save more money for financial security, retirement, or future purchases. It's time that we all leave the paycheck to paycheck lifestyles that are not pleasing to God, behind once and for all.

MIAD Holdings LLC. offers a biblical way to save for spiritual reasons. It is also painless and time-saving as well. A MIAD membership is a monthly membership/deposit directly from your paycheck, debit or credit card, or bank account. This deposit amount is then split and separated into several different accounts. This allows for safekeeping and acts as a tripwire to all the biblical principles that your accounts are designed to activate.

Your membership establishes your desire to understanding biblical and spiritual financial principles and to become a part of a family of members that are all working very hard to not only prove God's providence in the earth, but to also use wisdom in providing and protecting our own families.

ABOUT THE AUTHOR

I was born to Johnny Sidney Martin Sr. and Mary Ruth Martin in Atlanta, Ga. I grew up most of my life in Cincinnati, Ohio. After graduating High School, I didn't really know what I wanted to do with my life, but he knew I wanted to do something meaningful. So, while in college at the University of Cincinnati, I started praying for a career that was important. That's when I discovered that I wanted to become a Police Officer. After 10 years of Law Enforcement, one wife and two children, I tried my hand at business. 15 years later, at the age of 45, my purpose was revealed and the plan was established. I learned the value of a dollar at an early age from my hard-working parents. I understood how to earn my pay and even did ok with my savings, but I was a goal saver which means once my goal was reached, I would drain my savings and off I went to claim my prize. Though rewarding, this was no way to sustain me or my new family.

I then created MIAD Holdings LP. Is a Biblical Financial Literecy Program whose mission it is to fight poverty and eradicate lack. We teach the practical Biblical principles of stewardship, through a system of saving, borrowing, and lending that pulls people off the path of poverty once, and for all and plants them firmly on the path of real prosperity and abundance by Jesus Christ. I am convinced that Jehovah God wants to heal our land and that men and women like myself have been sent and given the Kingdom economic wisdom and instructions from Heaven to do. I am also married to my wonderful wife, Alvaun Martin, and the father of two wonderful daughters, Sydnie and Saundria Martin.

My Manifesto
I HAVE BEEN CROWNED BY GOD TO TEACH

HIS WORD

"For the word of God is quick, and powerful, and sharper than any two-edged sword, piercing even to the dividing asunder of soul and spirit, and of the joints and marrow, and is a discerner of the thoughts and intents of the heart."

Hebrews 4:12 KJV

LIFE

"He came that we might have life, and that they might have it more abundantly."

John 10:10 KJV

MATURITY

"When I was a child, I spake as a child, I understood as a child, I thought as a child: but when I became a man, I put away childish things."

1 Corinthians 13:11 KJV

NETWORKING

"From whom the whole body fitly joined together and compacted by that which every joint supplieth, according to the effectual working in the measure of every part, maketh increase of the body unto the edifying of itself in love."

Ephesians 4:16 KJV

BUSINESS

"Be kindly affectionate one to another with brotherly love; in honor preferring one another; Not slothful in business; fervent in spirit; serving the Lord;"

Romans 12:10,11 KJV

ATTITUDE

"But I say unto you, love your enemies, bless them that curse you, do good to them that hate you, and pray for them which despitefully use you, and persecute you;"

Matthew 5:44 KJV

Quick Start Guide

Make immediate changes in your life concerning your finances.

Confess & Repent

Armed with the understanding, and after searching the word of God with this new perspective of God being the only owner of everything, you must repent that you knowingly or unknowingly laid illegal claim to what was never yours to own, but only possess and steward over. Asking God to forgive you for your thieft's, and vow that you will steal no longer. Repent for your lack of understanding and for loving the gifts more than you love the giver.

Decree & Declare

Verbally confess that the earth is the Lord's, and everything it it. And mean it. Find scriptures that back up your confessions. The decree confession is the key to keeping both you and the Lord reminded of who has what responsibility in the relationship. By saying, "Lord, how would you like me to handle your business or how should I invest the savings you have instructed to me.

Actions

Prepare to let go of your most prized, if need be, at the leading of the Lord only. Many times, God has had me give away possessions that I accidentally became too fond of, for my own good. From an expensive watch to fine clothing. Begin to look at those objects that you once believed were yours, as God's and if He were to require a specific use of it, you would be more than willing and prepared to obey Him.

OPERATION RECOVER THE WEALTH BOOK SERIES

Thank You for Purchasing this Book.

Coming soon, nine more books in this series that are written and design to help you get the best understanding you possibly can, by focusing on one topic at a time. These are also great for teaching Bible study.

Contact Us

www.miadholdings.com
www.johnsidneymartin.com
www.blog.johnsidneymartin.com
www.getmiad.com

Follow Us

www.facebook.com/moneyisadefense
www.twitter.com/moneyisadefense
www.instagram.com/gmoneyisadefense
www.linkedin.com/in/moneyisadefense
www.youtube.com/channel/moneyisadefense

MIAD Holdings LLC
1106 Curtis Ave
Joliet, IL. 60435

Made in the USA
Middletown, DE
17 May 2021